DISCLAIMER

This work is an unofficial summary of the original book, *The Real Anthony Fauci* by Robert F. Kennedy Jr. It is written to capture the key points in the book and help the reader understand the main gist of the author. It features discussion questions, cover questions, and background information segments, making it an effective study material. Also, note that the content in this material isn't intended to replace the need for seeking independent professional help or advice when appropriate.

Just a Moment!

Download Your Free GIFT!

Just before you proceed, we have a valuable GIFT for you FREE of charge. Simply click HERE to get yours as soon as possible!

Alternatively, you can scan the QR code to access the download page

Table of Content

Background Information about the Author

Richard Francis Kennedy is an American lawyer and author. He is the son of U.S. Senator Robert F. Kennedy and a nephew to the former U.S. president, President J.F. Kennedy. He is a prominent anti-vaccine advocate and a vocal of Bill Gates, Anthony Fauci, Big Pharma and several other pro-vaccination entities. He is a professor of Environmental Law *at Pace University School of Law*. He is also a pioneering member of *Waterkeeper Alliance*, a non-profit environmental group.

Born in January 1954, Francis Kennedy was nine years old when his uncle, J.F Kennedy, was assassinated in 1963 and fourteen when his father was assassinated while running for president. Being from a politically-active home, he isn't without solid political opinions. For example, he was a prominent critic of President George Bush's environmental and energy policies, and he is a regular commentator on many U.S. political issues.

Kennedy is the chairman of *Children's Health Defense*. The group aims to address the plight of many American children suffering from varying health conditions. Under Kennedy's leadership, the group has campaigned against vaccines, paracetamol. Fluoridation of drinking water, wireless communication, etc.

Summary Overview

The Real Anthony Fauci by Richard F. Kennedy Jr. is a detailed appraisal of the conspiracies surrounding Anthony Fauci, Bill Gates, Big Pharma, et al. as well as the vaccine agenda. Kennedy carries out a meticulous examination of allegations, claims, events, researches, reports, etc., to expose the truths surrounding vaccines, pandemics, and of course, the recent COVID-19 pandemic.

Note to Readers

This summary is written in the first-person point of view, to capture and communicate the author's expression as accurately as possible. The reason for this summary technique is to give the readers a feel of the original book's structure. Enjoy!

Introduction

The governmental health regulations, media companies, and the idealistic population that most people rely on as champions of health, civil rights, democracy, freedom, and evidence-based public policy have all been compromised. Suddenly, they've seemed to be working together to generate fear, promote gullible obedience, and discourage critical thinking. With the manipulation of science, promotion of terror, and mass propaganda and censorship, they are engendering rising totalitarianism. The "emergency orders" that closed American businesses, schools, churches, etc. and other draconian laws imposed on Americans without legislative approval testify to this.

In the center of this mayhem is "the trusted public face of the United States government response to COVID," Dr. Anthony Fauci. I am a lifelong Democrat. My family "has had eighty years of deep engagement with America's public health bureaucracy and long friendships with key federal regulators, including Anthony Fauci, Francis Collins, and Robert Gallo." I also "built alliances with these individuals and their agencies during my years of environmental and public health advocacy." I admired them. But I also watched how the industry has transformed into a totalitarian entity over the years. My over 40 years of experience as an environmental and public health advocate exposed me to the "corrupting mechanisms of "regulatory capture, the process by which the regulator becomes beholden to the industry it's meant to regulate."

This book tracks Anthony Fauci's rise from his start as a young researcher into the powerful technocrat (that he is today) who has "helped orchestrate and execute 2020's historic coup d'état against Western democracy." It discusses medicine's monetization, which has left America's public health ailing and shattered its democracy. It also features the use of propaganda by the "mainstream media, Big Tech robber barons, the military and intelligence communities and their deep historical alliances with Big Pharma and public health agencies." Dr. Anthony Fauci was, however, in the center of all this.

Fauci, who turned eighty in 2020, has spent fifty years as America's reigning health commissar. All these proved to help him prepare for "his final role as Commander of history's biggest war against a global pandemic." Since 1968, he has occupied several posts in the *National Institute of Allergy and Infectious Diseases* (NIAID). He is paid $417,608 annual salary. This makes him the highest-paid of all federal employees, including the President. His tremendous experience garnered from his several years on the job and from advising Presidents, the Pentagon, intelligence agencies, foreign governments, and the WHO fully equipped him to wield so much power. Moreover, his assuring posture and attractive charisma amid Trump government during the pandemic helped him gain huge public trust.

Dr. Fauci's policies believed to deal with the pandemic, particularly the lockdowns, would later take a global relevance. It resulted in dire poverty, starvation, food insecurity, and crippled public health. For instance, "in 2020, disruptions to health and nutrition services killed 228,000 children in South Asia." In addition, untreated and undiagnosed terminal diseases accounted for thousands of lives. Fauci's business closures culminated in the most significant upward transfer of wealth in human history, pulverizing the middle-class to enrich the wealthy. "In 2020, workers lost $3.7 trillion while billionaires gained $3.9 trillion. Some 493 individuals became new billionaires, and an additional 8 million Americans dropped below the poverty line." The biggest winners of Fauci's lockdowns were the same companies supporting his policies and censoring his critics. These are the likes of Jeff Bezos, Bill Gates, Mark Zuckerberg, Eric Schmidt, Sergey Brin, Larry Page, Larry Ellison, and Jack Dorsey.

Dr. Fauci's eventual failure in achieving beneficial health outcomes during the COVID-19 pandemic is consistent with his failures during his fifty years running NIAID. Children born after his elevation to NIAID kingpin in 1984 have been described as the "sickest generation in American history." He has also contributed to making Americans one of the least healthy people on the planet, thanks to "his obsequious subservience to the Big Ag, Big Food, and pharmaceutical companies has left our children drowning in a toxic soup of pesticide residues, corn syrup, and processed foods."

Chapter 1: Mismanaging a Pandemic

I: Arbitrary Decrees: Science-Free Medicine

Dr. Fauci's first approach to curbing COVID-19 was to mandate the use of masks, social distancing, and lockdowns (which quarantines the healthy), and instructing COVID patients to return home and do nothing "until difficulties breathing sent them back to the hospital to submit to intravenous remdesivir and ventilation." This approach, of course, turned out to be grossly ineffective. Dr. Fauci and his Pharma collaborators suppressed treatments with the single intention to force Americans to seek salvation in the vaccines they intended to provide. This is why available, safe, and effective medicines were publicly rejected.

Common sense and scientific evidence showed that Dr. Fauci's approach was counter-productive as they caused far more deaths than they averted. He was aware that his mask mandates were contrary to overwhelming science. He had earlier dismissed the efficacy of mask use. He, however, denied this to Norah O'Donnell with *InStyle magazine*, stating that he was only trying to avoid the unavailability of masks to frontline workers "in the context of the time" in which he made his dismissal. His emails also reveal that he had been privately giving the same advice (dismissing the efficacy of masks). A February 5, 2020 email from him to Sylvia Burwell as to the futility of masking says:

> *A mask is much more appropriate for someone infected, and you're trying to prevent them from infecting other people than it is in protecting you against infection. If you look at the masks you buy in a drug store, the leakage around doesn't protect you. In the United States, there is absolutely no reason whatsoever to wear a mask.*

Dr. Fauci's sudden U-turn on the endorsement of masking "came at a time of increasing political polarization, and masks quickly became important tribal badges." This, combined with increased public fear, culminated in blind obedience and stifled general critical thinking. It became a tool of political expression. The lockdowns also rested on dubious scientific stances. In September 2021, FDA Commissioner Dr. Scott Gotleib maintained that "the six-foot distancing rule that Dr. Fauci and his HHS colleagues imposed upon Americans was "arbitrary," not, after all, science-backed." Besides, the WHO's official protocols had recommended against the lockdown of healthy people. But the relentless manipulation of data to support the vaccine agenda was also "became the apogee of a year of stunning regulatory malpractice."

Health officials, tasked with managing the pandemic, collaborated with mainstream media to censor dissenting views and critical public health questions to strengthen blind obedience rather than encourage honest, open, and responsible debate on the science. They silenced doctors who offered treatments that may compete with the vaccines or opposed the vaccine mandate. They shelved opposite stances under the shady cloak of "scientific consensus." Dr. Fauci's specialists, including President Biden and the network news anchors, advised Americans to "trust the experts." But, in reality, such a trust is undemocratic and anti-science. This is because science is dynamic, and "experts" often differ on scientific questions.

It turned out that Dr. Fauci's deceptive use of data aimed to arouse general fear and stir public desperation for the arrival of vaccines. Some of America's leading physicians and scientists who led the fight against the pandemic in the trenches have maintained that Fauci's obsessions with vaccines "prompted him to ignore or even suppress effective early treatments, causing hundreds of thousands of unnecessary deaths while also prolonging the pandemic." Dr. Peter McCullough is one of these doctors. He maintained that Fauci's approach of keeping seemed to pose much threat to public health. He argued that doctors could manage the disease by using "four to six drugs in combination, supplemented by vitamins and nutraceuticals including zinc, vitamins D and C, and Quercetin. And they can guide patients at home, even the highest-risk seniors, and avoid a Dreaded outcome of hospitalization and death."

At the start of the pandemic, Dr. David Brownstein confided in me: "I had a meeting with my staff and my six partners. I told them, 'We are going to stay open and treat COVID.' They wanted to know-how. I said, 'We've been treating viral diseases here for twenty-five years. COVID can't be any different. In all that time, our office had never lost a single patient to flu or flu-like illness. Our A, C, and D, and iodine. We administered IV solution outside all that time with IV hydrogen peroxide and vitamin C."

Meanwhile, he has seen many horrible vaccine side effects in their patients (who took the vaccines). In his words, "We've had seven strokes—some ending in severe paralysis. We had three cases of pulmonary embolism, two blood clots, two cases of Graves' disease, and one death."

Dr. Ryan Cole, the CEO/Medical Director of Cole Diagnostics, the largest independent lab in Idaho, expresses the highly life-saving value of early treatment. He performed over 125,000 COVID tests during the pandemic and has encountered many patients at the early stages of the disease. He provided early therapy to over 300 positive patients, "half of whom were comorbid and high risk." None of them was hospitalized, and none of them died.

In his words, "to not treat, especially amid a highly transmissible, deadly disease, is to harm." Now, Dr. Fauci's approach discouraged the early treatment of infected patients. Dr.

McCullough maintains that to have effectively controlled the pandemic, Dr. Fauci "should have created hotlines and dedicated websites for medical professionals to call in with treatment questions and to consult, collect, catalogue, and propagate the latest innovations for prophylaxis vulnerable and exposed individuals, and treating early infections, to avert hospitalizations." But Fauci's strategies only began when the under-medicated patients get hospitalized. He adopted the "unprecedented protocol of telling doctors to let patients diagnosed with a positive COVID test go home, untreated—leaving them in terror, and spreading the disease—until breathing difficulties forced their return to hospitals." This approach unwittingly prolonged the pandemic.

II: Killing Hydroxychloroquine

Dr. Fauci led the effort to derail Americans from life-saving drugs and available medicines, which might have saved many lives during the pandemic. This projects the intentions of the powerful vaccine cartel championed by Bill Gates and Dr. Fauci. The hydroxychloroquine (HCQ) and other therapeutics initially threatened Bill Gates and Dr. Fauci's $48 billion COVID vaccine project. The drug, remdesivir, in which Gates had a significant stake, was particularly hit. Under federal law, new medicines cannot qualify for Emergency Use Authorization (EUA) if any FDA-approved drug is effective against the same sickness.

Hence, if any FDA-approved drug-like hydroxychloroquine proved effective against COVID, the vaccine agenda would be legally crippled.

If hydroxychloroquine or ivermectin had been proven effective against the COVID vaccine, pharmaceutical companies would have been prevented from fast-tracking their billion-dollar vaccines. This would mean the vaccines "would have to endure the years-long delays that have always accompanied methodical safety and efficacy testing," which would result in less profit. Now, Dr. Fauci "invested $6 billion in taxpayer lucre in the Moderna vaccine alone", where he stands to collect a fortune in royalties (given the fact that his agency is co-owner of the patent). This explains why the mighty potentates targeted hydroxychloroquine (HCQ). President Trump's endorsement of HCQ on March 19, 2020, politicized the debate, thus giving Fauci's defamation campaign against the medicine some soft landing.

Fauci's argument that HCQ was dangerous was daunting, given the fact that the medicine "is a 65-year-old formula that regulators around the globe long ago approved as both safe and effective against a variety of illnesses." WHO, for decades, listed it as "proven effective against a long list of illnesses." Different generations have used it billions of times across the world. During my time in Africa, I took it as a preventive against malaria, just as many other African visitors did. African's call it "Sunday-Sunday" because millions of them take it religiously every week. In the U.S., the FDA had approved HCQ for 65 years. This meant physicians prescribed it for any off-label use, and the CDC deems it safe for pregnant women, breastfeeding women, children, infants, and the elderly.

Any existing therapeutic drug (with an expired patent) that could outperform any vaccine in dealing with COVID posed a threat to the pharmaceutical cartel. This explains why pharmaceutical interests "launched a multinational preemptive crusade to discredit HCQ far back in January 2020, months before the WHO declared a pandemic. On January 13, amidst the rumors of the Wuhan flu, the French government took the bizarre step of "reassigning HCQ from an over-the-counter to a prescription medicine." Then, without citing any study, they changed its status to "List II poisonous substance" and then banned its over-the-counter sales. Weeks later, the Canadian government did the same. A physician in Zambia reported that "organized groups of buyers emptied drugstores of HCQ and then burned the medication in bonfires outside the towns." In South Africa, two tons of life-saving hydroxychloroquine were destroyed in late 2020. Then, in 2021, the U.S. government ordered the destruction of more than a thousand pounds of HCQ.

By March 2020, frontline physicians reported miraculous results following early treatment with HCQ. For example, on March 13, Dr. James Todaro, M.D., a Michigan physician, "tweeted his review of HCQ as an effective COVID treatment, including a link to a public Google doc." But Google deleted Todaro's memo, giving users the impression that his information never existed. Google has a history of suppressing information that poses a challenge against the vaccine industry. This can be traced to the fact that Alphabet, her parent company, owns many vaccine companies.

Before the COVID pandemic, no single study had presented any evidence against the use of hydroxychloroquine (HCQ). It only began facing attacks when the news of its effectiveness against COVID-19 started to spread. By 2020, Bill Gates exercised firm control over WHO in his effort to discredit HCQ. In collaboration with Dr. Fauci, Bill Gates-influenced WHO "financed a cadre of research mercenaries to concoct a series of nearly twenty studies—all employing fraudulent protocols deliberately designed to discredit HCQ as unsafe."

Several studies which discredited the medicine were somehow connected to Gates and Dr. Fauci or other collaborators in the vaccine agenda. *The Lancet* and the *New England Journal of Medicine* (NEJM) also published fraudulent studies in a planned tirade against HCQ. Dr. Fauci and the vaccine cartel promptly responded by celebrating them on papers on May 22, 2020. Both studies "relied on data from the Surgisphere Corporation, an obscure Illinois-based "medical education" company that claimed to somehow control an extraordinary global database boasting access to medical information from 96,000 patients in more than 600 hospitals." This sketchy company was founded in 2008 and had eleven employees, including a science fiction writer and porn star/events hostess. But it claims to have data from six continents and hundreds of hospitals that administered HCQ to treat patients.

The fraudulent study from *Lancet* and *NEJM* could have held sway if not for 200 independent scientists who were quick to expose them, exposing the discrepancies in their "studies." One of these is the fact that "the number of reported deaths among patients taking hydroxychloroquine in one Australian hospital exceeded the total number of deaths for the entire country." The *New York Times* also reported that over "100 scientists and clinicians have questioned the authenticity" of the study. The *Lancet* would later give in to the pressure—three of their four co-authors finally requested that the paper be retracted. Both *Lancet* and *NEJM* eventually withdrew their papers. But, to date, neither the authors nor the journals have opened up on who induced them to come up with one of the biggest frauds in the history of scientific writing. *The Guardian* remarks on the publication and retraction thus: "The sheer number and magnitude of the things that went wrong or missing are too enormous to attribute to mere incompetence...What's incredible is that the editors of these esteemed journals still have a job."

III: Ivermectin

By the summer of 2020, frontline physicians discovered another COVID remedy that was as effective as HCQ. Two Merck scientists discovered Ivermectin (IVM) five years earlier, winning the Nobel Prize. IVM is known for its "unprecedented firepower against a wide range of human parasites, including roundworm, hookworm, river blindness, and lymphatic filariasis." It was, in 1996, approved by the FDA as fit for human use. WHO also recommended the use of IVM to treat people with parasitic infections.

And millions of people around the world have consumed billions of dozes with very minimal side effects recorded worldwide.

An April 2020 research by Australian researchers at Monash and Melbourne Universities maintained that IVM eliminates SARS-CoV-2 in cells in 48 hours. "Based on this study, on May 8, 2020, Peru—then under siege by a crushing COVID endemic— adopted ivermectin in its national guidelines." Their doctors were very familiar with the medicine, and the authorities knew it was safe for use. Its use in addressing COVID reduced COVID-related deaths in the country by 14 fold in the areas where the authorities had distributed the medicine. However, in December 2020, WHO prevailed over Peru's new president and caused him to reduce IVM availability, culminating in a 13 fold increase in COVID-related deaths. There were similar findings in Argentina and Bangladesh.

Since March 2020, over 20 randomized clinical trials (RCTs) "have confirmed its miraculous efficacy against COVID for both inpatient and outpatient treatment." Yale epidemiologist Dr. Harvey Risch, reacting to IVM treatment RTCs completed in 2021, maintained that all relevant studies "all showed significant benefit for high-risk outpatients." However, its performance only fell a little short in inpatients in the very late stages of COVID. In January 2021, Dr. David Chesler, a geriatric specialist who had treated 191 COVID-infected patients, wrote Fauci telling him "that he had achieved a mortality rate of 8 percent using ivermectin—half (and 146,000 deaths less than) the U.S. average in elder-care facilities." His letter featured documentation of a peer-reviewed case study on reports of the drug's similar effectiveness in other countries. But he got no reply from Dr. Fauci or anyone else from NIAID.

In late 2020, the news of the effectiveness of IVM was spreading. Now, Dr. Fauci et al. would have this. They needed to do something. The government began moving to block its use. On December 24, the South African government quietly banned the importation of ivermectin. YouTube removed Dr. Pierre Kory's video in which he testified for the effectiveness of the drug against COVID. Then, later in March 2021, "the US FDA, the European Medicines Association (EMA), and the WHO issued statements advising against the use of ivermectin for COVID-19. The EMA said it should not be used at all. The WHO..., said ivermectin's use should be limited to clinical trials..." and the FDA firmly argued that "You should not use ivermectin to treat or prevent COVID-19."

In response to the unreasonable action of the authorities in blacklisting IVM, in July 2021, "a front-page Wall Street Journal headline asked, "Why is the FDA Attacking a Safe, Effective drug?" Later, in September of the same year, the American Medical Association (AMA), the American Pharmacists Association (APhA), and the American Society of Health-System Pharmacists (ASHP) unanimously called on doctors to stop using ivermectin to treat COVID. Yet, Dr. Fauci, Bill Gates, Big Pharma, Big Tech, etc., were all out against it to discredit it before the public on some shady and untrue basis.

IV: Remdesiver

Dr. Fauci needed to use his "esoteric bureaucratic maneuvers mastered during his half-century at NIH" to secure FDA's approval for his vanity drug, remdesivir. Now, every legitimate study has shown that the drug has no effect against COVID. Worse still, it has been shown to be deadly and poisonous. Besides, it is very costly. At $3000, it is one thousand times more expensive than hydroxychloroquine and ivermectin. The ambition to promote his remdesvir prompted Dr. Fauci to sabotage HCQ and IVM. The FDA's recognition of HCQ and IVM would have threatened the remdesvir. He was aware of this fact.

By May 2020, doctors and hospitals began to use remdesivir on hospitalized patients of COVID-19. CDC website lists remdesivir and the corticosteroid dexamethasone as the only drugs approved for treating COVID, but assessing remdesivir's impact on COVID-19 patients is difficult because it causes extreme toxicity to lungs and kidneys just like COVID-19. Consequently, upon her dependency on the drug, the United States experienced double the number of deaths per month compared to other countries. Also, Brazil, one of the first nations to embrace the drug, had the second-highest death toll. Remdesiver turned out to be "a remedy worse than the malady."

V: Final Solutions: Vaccines or Bust

In the spring of 2020, Dr. Fauci and Bill Gates predicted that some "miraculous vaccine" would "stop transmission, prevent illness, end the pandemic." The apparent obstacle to this was that the coronavirus could rapidly mutate and produce vaccine-resistant variants. Hence, experienced "vaccine developers like Hotez and Offit doubted that... researchers could suddenly develop a COVID vaccine that would provide "sterilizing immunity," meaning that it would completely obliterate viral colonies in vaccinated individuals and prevent transmission and mutation." In line with this view, Britain's top vaccinologist, Andrew Pollard, admitted the failure of an Oxford University government-funded AstraZeneca vaccine to achieve sterilizing immunity in monkeys. Then, in August, Dr. Fauci, in a celebratory tone rather than in defeat, announced that none of the first-generation COVID vaccines was likely to prevent transmission.

Dr. Fauci and Bill Gates seemed to have the perfect solution. The two of them had committed billions of taxpayer and tax-deducted money into the development of an mRNA platform for vaccines "would allow them to quickly produce new "boosters" to combat each new "escape variant." Now, vaccines multiply profits by failing. Every new booster would double revenues from the initial jab. Since NIAID co-owned the mRNA patent, it stood to make billions from the scheme by producing successive boosters for every new variant. The more the booster, the more the profit. The goal was to make humanity dependent on biannual or triannual booster shots. Dr. Peter McCullough summed this up by stating that the leaky vaccine "would put the world on a never-ending booster treadmill."

An even more severe obstacle of coronavirus vaccines was their tendencies to "induce "pathogenic priming," known as "antibody-dependent enhancement" (ADE)—an overstimulation of immune system response that can cause severe injuries and death when vaccinated individuals subsequently encounter the wild viruses." In earlier experiments, coronavirus vaccines had tragically killed their recipients when exposed to wild viruses or made them vulnerable to harmful infections. Dr. Fauci and his confederates then came up with six strategies, all of which entailed hiding the evidence that ADE did occur if it did. By November 2021, they had largely succeeded in concealing the facts that Dr. Fauci's vaccines couldn't prevent the disease nor its transmission and that it was killing and injuring many Americans already. The relentless practice of frightening broadcasting news and purposefully inflating COVID deaths made most Americans look up to the vaccines for safety.

Many physicians and scientists have since complained that Dr. Fauci's vaccine promotions were "a vast, unprecedented population-wide experiment, with shady recordkeeping and no control group." Indeed, it was causing more death than it was averting. By October 6, US health officials had administered over "230 million doses of Pfizer's COVID vaccine, compared to 152 million doses of Moderna, and 15 million doses of Johnson & Johnson." Now, the final summary of Pfizer's six-month clinical trial data, which they submitted to the

FDA to win approval, revealed a key data point that should have impeded intervention forever: "far more people died in the vaccine group than in the placebo group during Pfizer's clinical trials." The fact that the FDA nevertheless granted them approval is clear proof that even the most dangerous medicine can make the public space, and the pharmaceutical industry and their government allies control public awareness through compliant physicians, media manipulation, etc.

Dr. Fauci and his allies began a deceptive campaign to claim credits for their jabs when deaths dropped in mid-December 2020. But, at this time, the Pfizer jab had only reached 8 percent of the population (27 million people). Besides, according to the CDC, the vaccine takes 60 days to provide protection, and the vaccination has only recently started. This quickly revealed the vaccination had very little if anything to do with the drop. Instead, the drop could be linked to the natural herd immunity given the spread of natural infections in the previous year and "the widespread use of ivermectin and hydroxychloroquine following Pierre Kory's December 5."

Almost all the countries that implemented rapid and aggressive vaccination experienced dramatic spikes in COVID infections. Here are a few instances:

In **Gibraltar**, where there was an aggressive vaccination of all 34,000 inhabitants, experienced a fivefold increase in infections and a nineteen-fold increase in death after vaccination.

Malta administered 800,000 doses to 500,000 inhabitants. But in early July 2021, the epidemic and fatalities surged, forcing the authorities to impose fresh restrictions and admitting that vaccination cannot shield people from COVID.

Eighty percent of **Iceland's** 360,000 inhabitants received one vaccine, while 75 percent of them had received two in July 2021. But, by mid-July, there was a massive surge in daily infections.

By June 2021, **Belgium** had vaccinated 75 percent of its 11.5 million inhabitants (with 65 percent having received two vaccinations). But, by July 2021, daily infections had risen from less than 500 to about 2,000. Their authorities admitted that vaccines couldn't stop or protect their citizens. Singapore vaccinated 80 percent of its population by the end of July 2021. But by late August 2021, the country experienced a spike in daily cases from about 10 to 150.

By July 2021, the **United Kingdom** had vaccinated 70 percent of its 67 million inhabitants. Still, by mid-July, they were experiencing 60,000 cases a day.

Despite the CDC's efforts to cover up the vaccine-related destruction in the United States, even the dysfunctional VAERS system records the unprecedented death rate following the vaccines. "Between December 14, 2020, and October 1, 2021, American doctors and bereaved families have reported more than 16,000 deaths and a total of 778,685 injuries to the *Vaccine Adverse Event Reporting System* (VAERS) following COVID vaccination." VAERS data shows a massive 69.84 spike in death rate two weeks after vaccination and 39.48 percent within 24 hours of the injections. VAERS also "recorded nearly 800,000 injuries by the 9½ months between December 14, 2020, and October 2021, with 112,000 classified as "serious." Pfizer underreported played down the severity of the massive injuries experienced during clinical trials. Bell's palsy, Guillain-Barré syndrome, multi-organ failure, amputation, blood clots, strokes, embolisms, blindness, etc., were reported during vaccination.

The legality of vaccinating children is also called in question. Studies have already shown that 600 children have died. Now, a recent Lancet study shows that a healthy child has no COVID risk; this suggests that these kids are dying unnecessarily. Furthermore, most children reacted adversely to the Pfizer COVID vaccine. One in nine of them suffered severe side effects rendering them unable to perform their activities. Hence, the idea of forcing the vaccine on healthy children is unethical.

Dr. Fauci gives the impression that the "unvaccinated" are more likely to spread the virus, suggesting that they shouldn't be allowed to live a normal civic life. But the error in this came to the fore in July 2021 when the CDC found out that "fully vaccinated individuals who contract the infection have as high a viral load in their nasal passages as unvaccinated individuals who get infected." Another study in Indonesia agrees with this observation upon discovering that "individuals carry 251x the viral loads of Delta and other mutant variants than they did in the pre-vaccine era." Another October 2021 investigation by Israel's medical authorities in Meir Medical Center in Sheba found that 23.3 percent of patients and 10.3 percent of staff infected got infected despite a 96.2 percent vaccination rate.

Chapter 2: Pharma Profits over Public Health

Throughout his fifty-year career, Dr. Anthony Fauci has built complex financial entanglements "among pharmaceutical companies, the National Institute of Allergy and Infectious Diseases (NIAID), and its employees that have transformed NIAID into a seamless subsidiary of the pharmaceutical industry." He has used his six million annual budget to control and dominate several agencies and governing bodies such as the CDC, FDA, HHS, WHO, UN, the Pentagon, and the White House. The yearly grants he gets empower him to make or break, punish, enrich university research centers, manipulate scientific research journals, and dictate the outcomes of scientific researches around the world.

Defense Advanced Research Projects Agency (DARPA) has, since 2005, "funneled an additional $1.7 billion3 into Dr. Fauci's annual discretionary budget to launder suspicious and sketchy funding for biological weapons research. With his close relationship with bid pharmaceuticals and other large grantmakers like Bill Gates (the biggest funder of vaccines in the world), Dr. Fauci often uses his power to bully, control, and silence scientists whose research threatens his pharmaceutical paradigm and reward scientists who support his agenda. He "rewards loyalty with prestigious sinecures on key HHS committees when they continue to advance his interests." His control over these panels helps him deal with regulatory hurdles and skip critical milestones such as animal testing.

Under his watch as America's Health Czar, Dr. Fauci has massively contributed in a world in which Americans pay the most for medicines but experience the worst health outcomes compared to other wealthy nations. Unfortunately, under his management, NIAID has become massively plagued by corruption. He has "implemented a system of.... transactional culture that has made NIAID a seamless appendage of Big Pharma." NIAID lap researchers supplement their income with the honoraria they receive from attending Pharma seminars and sharing inside information about research progress with pharmaceutical companies. These officials defend this practice with the point that pharmaceutical dollars help strengthen NIAID's labs and allow the agency to retain staff. All this explains why "a 2004

Office of Government Ethics investigation chided Dr. Fauci for failing to control the corrupting entanglements between his staffers and pharmaceutical companies."

Since Dr. Fauci arrived at NIH, the agency has spent $856.90 billion. Also, every drug (from210 different pharmaceuticals) approved by the FDA between 2010 and 2016 originated from research funded fully or partly by NIH. After drug approval, Dr. Fauci collaborates with his pharmaceutical partners on promoting and profiting from their new products at the expense of taxpayers and consumers. For example, he "launched his career by allowing Burroughs Wellcome (now GlaxoSmithKline) to charge $10,000 annually for azidothymidine (AZT), an antiretroviral medication developed exclusively by NIH and tested and approved by Dr. Fauci himself." He knew that the product cost was mere $5/dose to manufacture. But then, "higher profit for industry "partners" often means more extravagant royalty payments for his NIAID and NIH cronies."

Remdesivir, the drug developed by Dr. Fauci himself, is a more recent example. While it proved ineffective against COVID, Dr. Fauci manipulated normal protocols to create the illusion of efficacy. He stood against opposition from FDA and WHO and declared from the White House that remdesvir would be effective against COVID, thus opening it up for the global market. Then Gilead sold remdesivir for $3,300–$5,000 per dose while the raw materials for producing a dose only cost them under $10. Fauci ignored this. He has made himself "the leading angel investor of the pharmaceutical industry." The NIH, NIAID, CDC, and FDA have become "pharmaceutical marketing machines" to him. All these have taken a toll on American health and democracy.

Chapter 3: The HIV Template for Pharma Profiteering

On December 4, 1940, Anthony Fauci was born in Brooklyn's Dyker Heights. Three of his grandparents were native Italians. The four of them came to the US at the end of the nineteenth century. His parents were both born in New York City. His father, Stephen Fauci, graduated from the College of Pharmacy, Columbia University, and his mother, Eugenia, went to Brooklyn College and Hunter College. Since his father was a pharmacist, Dr. Fauci's parents owned a drugstore. While his father filled prescriptions, his mother was the cashier.

Dr. Fauci attended Our Lady of Guadeloupe Grammar School in Brooklyn and Regis High School. He was a good athlete and particularly active in Basketball. Speaking to Wall Street, one of his old classmates, John Zeman, describes him as "a ball of fire" who "would literally dribble through a brick wall." In 1958, he went to Holy Cross College, where he studied philosophy, French, Greek, and Latin and graduated with a BA in 1962. However, he never doubted that he wanted to be a doctor right from High School. In 1966, he got his medical degree from Cornell 1966 where he graduated with a first-class. Upon completing his residency at Cornell Medical Center, he joined NIH in 1968 as a clinical associate at the NIAID and became deputy clinical director of NIAID in 1977.

When Dr. Fauci got aboard NIAID leadership, "allergic and autoimmune disorders were hardly a factor in American life." Autoimmune diseases were also rare occurrences. Most Americans had never seen a child with autism. The swine flu and America's response to it were marred by corruption cases similar to what we see today. CDC Director David Sencer, NIAID chief Richard Krause, among others, were accused of profiting off dangerous vaccines at the expense of public health. Richard Krause resigned in 1984 while Dr. Fauci took over from him. Dr. Fauci's lesson from the swine flu crisis "seems to have been the revelation that pandemics were opportunities of convenience for expanding agency power and visibility, and for cementing advantageous partnerships with pharmaceutical behemoths and for career advancement."

Four years later, the AIDS pandemic proved to be the opportunity for his stellar rise. The lessons he learned from dealing with the AIDS crisis "would become familiar templates for managing subsequent pandemics." He spent the next half a century shaping public responses to real and concocted pandemics like the SARS in 2003, bird flu in 2005, dengue in 2012, etc. He became skilled at exaggerating the potency of contagions to spread fear. During the AIDS crisis, in speaking of the disease, he once said: "something less than truly intimate contact can give you this disease." But in reality, it turned out that there is never any case of AIDS spreading by ordinary close contact.

Dr. Fauci's ability to combine charm and flattery with misinformation and misdirection to sway the media into suspending skepticism is a major factor, while Fauci has gone away with so much. Kramer observed in 1987 that the reason for this is that "is that he's attractive and handsome and dapper and extremely well-spoken and he never answers your question." Celia Farber, a veteran AIDS reporter on Fauci, also says: "...he is a revolutionary—a very dangerous one, who slipped behind the gates when nobody understood what he was bringing in. What was he bringing in? He was bringing in—as a trained Jesuit and committed Globalist—a new motion that would achieve all aims for Pharma and the powers he served."

The PIs: The Pharma/Fauci Mercenary Army

Given NIAID's lack of in-house drug development capacity, Dr. Fauci built his program "by farming out drug research to a network of so-called "principal investigators" (PIs) to control pharmaceutical companies. Acting as lobbyists, spokespersons, liaisons, and enforcers, PIs serve as "the glue that holds" pharmaceutical companies, hospital systems, HMOs and insurers together. The group comprises "powerful academic physicians and researchers who use federal grants and pharmaceutical industry contracts to build feudal empires at universities and research hospitals that mainly conduct clinical trials... for new pharmaceutical products." Through NIAID (which serves as a tiny part of its network), PIs determine the direction of America's biomedical research.

PIs members use their prominence across medical boards and chairmanships of university departments to propagate heresy, silence criticisms, and censor dissenting views. They have form control over the Data and Safety Monitoring Boards (DSMBs), Vaccines and Related Biological Products Advisory Committee (VRBPAC), The Advisory Committee on

Immunization Practices (ACIP), etc. This gives them the wherewithal to influence the outcomes of clinical trials, shape public perception on what vaccines are safe or aren't, and so much more.

Dr. Fauci and his Pharma partners "use their PIs to control the key FDA and CDC panels that license and "recommend" new vaccines for addition to the childhood schedule." Hence, NIAID contributes to funding them (the PIs). Dr. Fauci does this under the tag of funding "for drug development was an abdication of the agency's duty to find the source and eliminate the explosive epidemics of allergic and autoimmune disease." The PIs are also funded by "rich contracts from big drug companies and drug products' royalty payments." Many pharmaceutical companies buy the PIs' loyalty and support this way. Dr. Fauci's experience as a scientist and administrator helped him leverage the influence of the PIs at first. But he would later advance beyond this stage to command and organize the group "into a powerful juggernaut that journalist John Lauritsen calls "the Medical Industrial Complex."

Chapter 4: The Pandemics Template: AIDS and AZT

The process towards the approval of the AZT created the atmosphere for Dr. Fauci to pioneer and perfect corrupt, deceitful, and bullying practices that would become the order of the day over the next thirty-three years "to transform NIAID into a drug development dynamo." When he entered into the principal investigator drug-testing universe, Burroughs Wellcome was the only pharmaceutical company that "had a drug candidate teed up to test as an AIDS remedy—a toxic concoction, azidothymidine, known popularly as "AZT." US government-financed researchers had developed the drug in 1964 as leukemia chemotherapy. It works by destroying DNA synthesis in reproducing cells. FDA later abandoned it after it proved lethal and ineffective. It proved too toxic even as cancer chemotherapy.

In 1985, Samuel Broder, head of the National Cancer Institute (NCI), and his team and colleagues at Duke University discovered AZT killed HIV in test tubes. This "inspired Burroughs Wellcome to retrieve AZT from Horwitz's scrap heap and patent it as an AIDS remedy." Recognizing the desperation of dying AIDS patients, they "set the price at up to $10,000/year per patient—making AZT one of the most expensive drugs in pharmaceutical history." But, in reality, they spent pennies on manufacturing cost per dose. Nevertheless, AZT proved irresistible for Fauci in his desire to "anoint his new regime with the patina of competence." Burroughs Wellcome's PIs gradually dominated NIAID's clinical trial system, influencing NIH's key drug selection committee. With this, they could determine AZT's competition.

Dr. Fauci would replicate this system "to populate key drug and vaccine approval committees in FDA, CDC, and at the Institute of Medicine (IOM) with his Pharma PIs, giving him, and his Pharma partners, complete, vertically integrated control over the drug approval process from molecule to market." But, for some reason, it didn't immediately turn out as easy as he probably expected. He couldn't populate any clinical trial of any competing drug. For three years, NAIAD couldn't produce any approved effective alternative.

Meanwhile, several community-based AIDS doctors were springing in cities like Los Angelis, San Francisco, etc., and had become specialists in treating AIDS symptoms. They were largely successful with "therapeutic drugs that seemed effective against the constellation of symptoms that killed and tormented people with AIDS." These drugs included "off-the-shelf remedies like ribavirin, alpha interferon, DHPG, Peptide D, and Foscarnet for retinal herpes...." But Dr. Fauci refused to test any of these drugs that had expired or older patents and had no Pharma patrons. This created a situation where people with AIDS and community doctors purchased these remedies from underground buyers' clubs."

When every attempt to establish a worthy alternative failed, Dr. Fauci cut Burroughs Wellcome PIs every courtesy to accelerate AZT's approval at the company's mercy. He compromised the strict examination such a toxic drug was supposed to have been subjected to. He also endorsed the scheme to price AZT at an exorbitant $10,000 per patient per year. Thirty-six years later, he would repeat the same practice to ensure the approval of his drug, remdesivir, and Moderna's coronavirus vaccine. Fauci's compromise with Burroughs Wellcome and AZT utterly put him at the company's mercy and aided the AZT-only agenda. As a result, more people had contracted the AIDS virus for years, and there was no safe remedy.

By 1987, Dr. Fauci's political partners, both within and outside his party, had realized he had failed on the AIDS drug issue. This included Senator Kennedy and President Ronald Regan. In 1988, his "congressional sponsors turned on him during a dramatic Capitol Hill confrontation," demanding that he explain his slow progress. California Congresswoman Nancy Pelosi, among others, lamented his slow pace. She once put him on the spot by asking him: "You know the theory behind aerosol pentamidine to prevent pneumonia is strong. You know that the aerosol pentamidine was evaluated by the NIH as highly promising. You know that many studies in San Francisco recommend it routinely and that it is available. . . . Would you take aerosol pentamidine or would you wait for a study?" Now, for years, Fauci had denied the effectiveness of the drug to people with AIDS. He admitted to Pelosi that he would take the drug if he "already had a bout of Pneumocystis." He did this in the presence of an audience aware that he never tested or recommended the drug, denying people with AIDS access to remedies. This revealed his character.

Larry Kramer was one of the most vocal critics of Fauci over the Capitol Hill incident. His main grouse was how he (Fauci) kept quiet about such information for so long. "There are more AIDS patients dead because you didn't test drugs on them," Kramer charged at Fauci. This and many more criticisms spurred Fauci to plot a strategic pivot. Once, "he accosted Larry Kramer on a Montreal street during an international AIDS conference, took him for a walk, effectively begged forgiveness, and proposed a working partnership." He also began testing AIDS community drugs. He partnered with front-line AIDS doctors, giving them the authority and money to launch a local Community Research Initiative (CRI) and test promising drugs. By 1989, he became passionate about speeding up drug testing and approval to address AIDS and all life-threatening illnesses.

Fauci's sudden U-turn would later strain his relationship with his PIs. This was putting them at his mercy. However, his whole charade came to an end the moment FDA approved AZT. Then, he "had rigged the key committees that controlled drug approvals at NIH and FDA by stacking them with academic and industry scientists and doctors from his PI system." Government researchers had thoroughly accessed the drug and found it to be toxic. But, under Burroughs Wellcome's heavy finance, Dr. Fauci's trials worked used a fragmented study group "in twelve cities into small cohorts, making safety signals difficult to detect." He cut the proposed six-month human study duration to four months, making it even more difficult for researchers to detect side effects of the drug.

Following the manipulated, brief clinical trials, the FDA granted AZT Emergency Use Approval in March 1987. This was, for Dr. Fauci, something to show after his earlier humiliation. At this point, he called the press conference (something he loves to do) to announce the "feat." Upon his announcement, "Burroughs Wellcome's shares soared 45 percent... adding 1.4 billion pounds to the company's UK stock market value in one day." The company's CEO predicted that the AZT would bring in over $2 billion yearly. The company had given Dr. Fauci "a blockbuster AIDS Drug" and "a tried-and-tested system for producing future drug approvals." Nevertheless, his entire clinical trial for the "successful" AZT had been a fraud. This would spell some trouble for him in the coming years.

The AZT came under a series of scrutiny from scientists and the press. John Lauritsen, an investigative journalist who had covered the AIDS crisis in 1985, was the first intrepid journalist to examine the details of the AZT trials. He found the research to be invalid. He found it "marred by contradictions, ill-logic, and special pleading." The FDA had investigated the study. But, for many months, they cowered before Fauci's bullying and kept the reports secret. But Lauritsen stumbled upon five hundred pages from the FDA reports. They showed that "the Fauci/Burroughs Wellcome research teams had engaged in widespread data tampering, which some have viewed rose to the level of homicidal criminality." Many other scientists also lent their voice to this discovery. But all efforts to get Dr. Fauci to answer his critics failed. He declined several interviews, including some from NBC and BBC.

Despite his ineptitude and failures, Dr. Fauci has managed to survive "by cultivating credulous journalists who do not ask critical questions and give him free rein to broadcast self-serving propaganda." He has also mastered the practice of convincing media outlets not to give platforms to his critics. This was effective for him in 2020 and 2021. This recently came to play in how he silenced pop icon Nicki Minaj after questioning whether the vaccine might cause testicular swelling, among other problems. When asked about this accusation on CNN, he declared, "the answer to that, Jake, is a resounding no," with no study to support his assertion (as typical of him). But the vaccine manufacturers admitted that the vaccines weren't tested for effects on fertility. Not too long later, Twitter censored Minaj's communication. It didn't end there, "Pharma's obedient attack dogs CNN, CBS, and NBC rushed... to defame and discredit the rapper and to assure the public that Minaj was wrong."

Chapter 5: The HIV Heresies

Around four hundred years ago, after Galileo, politics and power continued to dictate scientific consensus instead of critical thinking and empiricism. This has constantly threatened democracy and public health. The same philosophy is expressed through phrases like "trust the experts." It paints an illusion of a "settled science," which, in itself, is an oxymoron. Science isn't settled but "disruptive, irreverent, dynamic, rebellious, and democratic." Hence, appeals to authority (CDC, WHO, Anthony Fauci, Bill Gates, etc.) is a feature of religion and not science.

Contrary to what they would have us believe, empirical truths arise from debates, questioning, skepticism, etc. Hence, the idea of consensus science is an illusion. If something is science, it isn't consensus.

The foundational issues surrounding AIDS is "an illustration of how vested interests (in this case, Dr. Anthony Fauci), using money, power, position, and influence, can engineer consensus on incomplete theories, and then ruthlessly suppress dissent." Many critics have offered logical analysis and views challenging the official orthodoxy that HIV causes AIDS. No one, however, has been able to come up with a convincing scientific proposition for this accepted orthodoxy. Instead, it is plagued with incoherence, knowledge gaps, contradictions, and inconsistencies but concealed under the umbrella of consensus.

Instead of answering critics and clearing the air on controversial issues like the HIV/AIDS debate, Dr. Fauci has "a theology that denounces questioning of his orthodoxy as irresponsible, uninformed, and dangerous heresy." His ability to censor and ultimately silence prominent dissidents is hitch-free. Anyone who dares question any of his canons that promote the orthodoxy that HIV is the one and only cause of AIDS becomes an enemy to be censored and silenced. With his control of the press, he bullies, intimidates, and vilifies his critics, and tries to bury their stances. The most prominent challenge on his stance on HIV/AIDS came from Dr. Peter Duesberg.

First, Duesberg accuses Fauci of committing mass murder with AZT, which, according to him, never cures. But his critic went deeper to state that "HIV does not cause AIDS but is simply a "free rider" common to high-risk populations who suffer immune suppression due to environmental exposures." He states that while HIV may be sexually transmittable, AIDS isn't. He argues that "HIV is seen in millions of healthy individuals who never develop AIDS. Conversely, there are thousands of known AIDS cases in patients who are not demonstrably infected with HIV." Many other scientists have similarly argued that "HIV plays a role in the onset of AIDS but argue that there must be other cofactors, a qualifier that Dr. Fauci and a handful of his diehard PIs stubbornly deny." In his 1987 article titled *Cancer Research* and in his book, *inventing the AIDS virus*, Duesberg exposes the flaws in Dr. Fauci's HIV/AIDS hypothesis. Dr. Fauci never answered.

While I take no side in this dispute, it seems that the dissidents have presented legitimate concerns that warrant some response, research, or exploration. Still, Dr. Fauci's unwavering silence to these only arouses suspicion. His hypothesis had been wholly inherited from Dr. Robert Gallo, a National Cancer Institute (NCI) researcher who is believed to have discovered the virus. Gallo himself had stolen the accolade from French virologist Luc Montagnier.

Chapter 6: Burning the HIV Heretics

In 1991, seven years after Dr. Robert Gallo's hypothesis on HIV/AIDS, Dr. Charles Thomas organized prominent experts in virologists and immunology to register an objection to Gallo's hypothesis. The group included the likes of Dr. Walter Gilbert of Harvard; PCR inventor Kary Mullis; Yale mathematician Serge Lang; Dr. Harry Rubin, professor of Cell Biology at UC Berkeley; Dr. Harvey Bialy, cofounder of *Nature Biotechnology*; Bernard Forscher, Ph.D., ret. Editor of *Proceedings of the National Academy of Sciences*, among others. They were asking for an open debate and investigation, and this was reasonable. But Dr. Fauci and Big Pharma used their influence to prevail over medical journals to decline to publish the request letter of these scientists. These journals relied on the pharmaceutical industry for up to 90 percent of their revenues. *Lancet* editor Richard Horton right observed that "the journals have devolved into information laundering operations for the pharmaceutical industry."

The steady flow of money from NAIAD strengthened Gallo's hypothesis "into an ironbound orthodoxy." The government virologist and pharmaceutical had taken hold of it to keep the income coming. As Dr. Charles Thomas puts it, "They've got to hold onto HIV. Why? To hold on to their funding." Professor Peter Duesberg was among the experts who challenged Gallo's orthodoxy. He was a demigod in molecular biology. He was one of the most respected scientists of his time. At the University of California, he "became the first to map the genetic structure of retroviruses like HIV, making him among the world's most renowned retrovirologists." In 1970, when he was thirty-three, he won acclaim for discovering the first cancer-causing gene. This discovery sprung the "mutant gene theory." But his belief that scientists ought to question every orthodoxy (including theirs) led him to subject his "oncogene theory to more rigorous tests than had any of its critics." Upon his research, he concluded that his discovery had been a fluke.

Duesberg was "committed to clean functional proof" at a time when Biology was about the discovery of new viruses. At that time, "pharmaceutical companies were minting profits from a pharmacopeia of patented antivirals devised by isolating these viruses and identifying compounds that could kill them. Every research scientist was aware of the

Nobel committee's bias toward breakthroughs that boosted Pharma's profit potentials." Duesberg had always found Gallo's hypothesis incoherent. It didn't make sense to him that an ancient retrovirus would attack its human host. Upon Gallo's announcement, Duesberg spent the next eighteen months "studying every scientific publication on HIV and AIDS." He eventually noted, among other things, that Gallo's claim that HIV caused leukemia, and later, AIDS, was incoherent, considering the fact that leukemia is the cellular opposite of AIDS. He argued that HIV is incapable of causing cancer or AIDS, but a "harmless passenger virus" that has existed with humans for thousands of generations.

Duesberg's arguments are compelling, irresistible, and clean. His challenge to Gallo and Fauci's HIV-only hypothesis stirred an expectation for a response. But Dr. Fauci and AIDS cartel ignored it and criticized anyone who credited it. Dr. Fauci made Duesberg an example to discourage future dissidents. He orchestrated a series of vicious attacks that eventually ended Duesberg's career. He "summoned the entire upper clergy of his HIV orthodoxy—and all of its lower acolytes and altar boys—to unleash a storm of fierce retribution on" Duesberg and his followers in what would come to be recognized as "one of the most sensational... personalized battles in the history of science." Dr. Fauci had a stake in this. His career depended on the hypothesis that HIV alone causes AIDS. Under Fauci's leadership, the medical carted subjected to heavy criticism. The NIH defunded him. The academia ostracized him. The scientific press also burnished the brilliant Berkeley professor.

Dr. Fauci controls all the levers of power and public opinion. He used this massively against Duesberg on every front. Before 1987 when Dr. Fauci took action against him, the NIH had never rejected a single one of Peter Duesberg's proposals. Celia Farber observed this reality thus: "The US military-industrial complex—HHS, NIH, NCI, DAIDS—all of it, is designed along with military command structure because it is... It is the military. It's not 'science,' and it's not 'merit.' Fauci understands this and has mastered eliminating both dissent and any mercy for the destroyed. It's a sin, as he has now openly said, to question him—to question 'science."

Chapter 7: Dr. Fauci, Mr. Hyde: NIAID's Barbaric and Illegal Experiments on Children

Since Dr. Anthony Fauci took over the National Institute of Allergy and Infectious Diseases (NIAID), he has often treated America's most vulnerable kids as collateral damage. AZT's shady and corrupt approval in 1988 opened up "a multibillion-dollar boom in new HIV drugs." Consequently, Dr. Fauci allowed his pharmaceutical partners and PIs to conduct unethical human experiments, exposing children and adults to toxic compounds. The HHS and the Public Health Service, its predecessor, already had a long history of carrying out unethical experiences on vulnerable subjects like institutionalized adults, imprisoned convicts, adults with intellectual disabilities, orphaned children, etc.

In vaccine campaigns, government regulators and pharma partners often combine child abuse with racial discrimination. For example, US vaccinologists Hilary Koprowski and Stanley Plotkin, during the 1950s and 60s polio vaccine experiments, "worked with Belgian colonial authorities in the Congo to recruit millions of Black African child "volunteers" for dozens of mass population trials with experimental vaccines that were perhaps considered to be too risky to test on white children." 1989, the CDC conducted dangerous experiments with a toxic measles vaccine on Black kids in Cameroon, Haiti, and South-Central Los Angeles. The experiment ended up killing dozens of little kids before it was halted.

Dr. Fauci's corrupt collaboration with pharmaceutical companies which yielded the AZT's scandalous approval in 1987, strengthened his relationship with Pharma's PIs. This relationship gave birth to several opportunities, causing Dr. Fauci to overlook Pharma's excesses. The 1980 Bayh–Dole Act allowed him "to file patents on the hundreds of new drugs that his agency-funded PIs were incubating, and then to license those drugs to pharmaceutical companies and collect royalties on their sales." This enterprise dwarfed HHS' regulatory functions and kept colossal money coming in.

The huge NIH and NIAID profit made clinical trials a booming industry. Vera Sharav, a holocaust survivor, spent her career investigating NIAID's abusive human experiments. She confided in me that "beginning around 1990, clinical trials became the profit center for the medical community... The most ambitious doctors left patient care and gravitated toward clinical trials. Everybody involved was making money except the subjects of the human experiments. At the center of everything were NIH and NIAID. While people were not paying attention, the agency quietly became the partner of the industry." Pharma's ethics had corrupted NAIAD's culture.

Investigative journalist Liam Scheff, in 2004, maintained that Dr. Fauci, in a bid to develop the second generation of profitable AIDS drug as an encore to AZT, "turned Black and Hispanic foster kids into lab rats, subjecting them to torture and abuse in a grim parade of unsupervised drug and vaccine studies." In his words, "the drugs being given to the children are toxic—they're known to cause genetic mutation, organ failure, bone marrow death, bodily deformations, brain damage, and fatal skin disorders." Many of these turned out fatal. Several of the kids suffered various degrees of permanent body damage.

In 2004, BBC hired investigative reporter Celia Farber to research a heartbreaking documentary chronicling the "savage barbarism of Dr. Fauci's science projects" on children. In the film, Celia is quoted thus:

> "I found the mass grave at Gate of Heaven Cemetery in Hawthorne, New York. It was a very large pit with AstroTurf thrown over it, which you could actually lift up. Under it one could see dozens of plain wooden coffins, haphazardly stacked. There may have been 100 of them. I learned there was more than one child's body in each. Around the pit was a semi-circle of several large tombstones on which upward of one thousand Children's names had been engraved. I wrote down every name. I'm still wondering who the rest of those kids were. As far as I know, nobody has ever asked Dr. Fauci that haunting question... This story ran in the NY Post, believe it or not. But one after the other, every media outlet that touched this story got cold feet. Even then, the medical cartel had this power to kill this kind of story. Dr. Fauci has built his career on that attitude."

The same year, AP Reporter John Solomon also investigated how many children died during Dr. Fauci's AIDS experiments. He found out that "at least 465 NYC foster children were subjects in NIAID's trials and that Dr. Fauci's agency provided fewer than one-third (142) of those children with an advocate—the minimum legally mandated protection." In addition, he found out that NAIAD carried out at least forty-eight AIDS experiments in seven states in violation of the federal requirement that each of them should be provided with an advocate.

As always, Dr. Fauci has managed to put-up highly pretentious cover-ups that "his experiments were compassionate gestures to impoverished orphans was always a sham. NIAID's claim that their experiments were the only opportunity for those children to receive "life-saving" drugs was a canard from the outset." In his 2004 article, *Inside Incarnation*, Liam Scheff suggests that Dr. Fauci and his PIs took advantage of the fact that Incarnation Children's Center is a non-medical facility to carry out exercises that experienced professional doctors or nurses would tag illegal. When children refused toxic drugs, they would surgically implant feeding tubes in their bellies to force the drugs into their systems. The more children resisted the drugs or threw up on taking them, the more feeding tubes NIAID and its Pharma partners came brought into the facility. This cost many kids their lives.

In 2005, the NYC Administration of Child Services (ACS) commissioned a report by Vera Institute. The Vera Institute Report is the result of a twenty-year investigation into Dr. Fauci's NIAID AIDS experiments predominantly featuring African American and Latino children in foster care. The report, among other facts, found out that: eighty of 532 children used in clinical trials died, 25 children died while enrolled in a medication trial, "64 children participated in thirty medication trials that were, against the required policy, NOT REVIEWED by a special medical advisory panel, etc.

Chapter 8: White Mischief: Dr. Fauci's African Atrocities

Racism is a feature of medical authoritarianism. This is often characterized in narratives around diseases reeking racial bigotries. The editor of the Nature Biotechnology journal, Harvey Bialy, observed that "the fearful fascination with the contagion was amplified by the official narrative that the disease originated in Africans doing weird things with monkeys, and spread to the voodoo kingdom of Haiti, and that the sexual depravity of homosexuals drove the disease into the United States." Charles Ortleb, the editor of *New York Native* also maintained the same stance in his words that "there was always this undertone of bigotry with AIDS."

Journalist Celia Farber also makes a similar observation stating that "The racism is cloaked inside carefully crafted philanthropic manipulations such as 'access' to drugs. It's never access to clean drinking water, education, sanitation, nutrition." This, for her, is created with the pictures that Africans are so sick and that "we have the drugs to 'save' their lives." Eventually, when the opposite happens, it's hidden under the "false front of charity." She describes this as *Pharma colonialism*. Africa has, for long, been a pharma colony, and the choice of companies that seek "cooperative government officials, compliant population, the lowest per-patient cost," etc. The powerless and often illiterate volunteers "to paper over even catastrophic side effects and mistakes." In line with this fact, the FDA, in 2005, observed that "Dr. Fauci's DAIDS team had concealed scores of deaths and hundreds of injuries during HIV drug trials in Africa with another of his toxic product, Nevirapine."

During George W. Bush's administration, Dr. Fauci told the president that HIV had taken over Africa and persuaded him to redirect US foreign aid into eliminating AIDS in Africa. In January 2002, the president obliged him by announcing "a $15 billion package to combat AIDS, including a $500 million program to purchase millions of doses of Nevirapine for distribution to African mothers and children." With these funds, DAIDS sponsored the test "the efficacy and safety of Nevirapine and AZT on preventing maternal transmission of HIV to newborns" in Uganda. The study was successful in the open but was marred with glaring methodological deficiencies. Fauci convinced the WHO to grant the drug Emergency Use Authorization Approval (EUA) based on this marred study. He persuaded President Bush to purchase millions of dollars of it with this done. Eventually, cartons of these ineffective drugs were shipped into fifty-three developing nations. All this was done to promote the drug, fetch-in profit, at the expense of the health of the African people who took the drug.

The pharmaceutical and the medical cartel have always preferred the people of color to test dangerous drugs. For example, in 1992, the *Los Angelis Times* revealed that the CDC regularly conducted "unlicensed experiments with a deadly flu vaccine on Black children in Haiti and Cameroon...." This explained why Blacks at that time were unwilling to sign-up for clinical trials. Only 4 percent of those who enrolled for clinical trials were Black.

Chapter 9: The White Man's Burden

Following Dr. Gallo's press conference in 1984, Dr. Fauci promised the world an AIDS vaccine. He thought a functioning AIDS immunization would silence Duesberg and other critics. Consequently, he "pumped our money into nearly 100 vaccine candidates, with none of these coming even close to the finish line." Eventually, in 2019, quite surprisingly, he announced that he finally had a working vaccine. This was months before the COVID-19 pandemic. While the vaccine had demonstrated a "bare 30 percent efficacy in human trials in Thailand, data from the Phase III trial in South Africa looked promising, and NIAID was getting teed up to test the vaccine on Americans."

Dr. Robert Redfield worked as Donald Trump's CDC director during the COVID-19 pandemic. Dr. Deborah Birx also served on Tramp's coronavirus task force. Both doctors were Army medical officers who led the military AIDs research. US military documents showed that, in 1992, when both doctors were serving in Walter Reed in Washington, they published inaccurate data claiming that an HIV vaccine they helped develop was effective. They must have known the vaccine was worthless. Later on, upon being threatened with being court-martialed and the revocation of his medical license, "Dr. Redfield confessed to angry DOD interrogators and the tribunal that his analyses were faulty and deceptive. He agreed to correct them and to publicly admit the vaccine was worthless at an upcoming AIDS conference at which he was scheduled to speak in July 1992." But, instead of retracting his lies in subsequent international HIV conferences, he promoted it passionately. This worked!

Redfield's gamble caused Congress to appropriate $20 million to the military to support Redfield and Birx's project. Congress' commitment impeded the initial intention of military prosecutors to court-martial Redfield. This incident catapulted Birx and Redfield to the apex of their careers. They became top federal health officials. Gallo's later partnership with Redfield became an instant success. The IHV report in 2017 expressed that the two of them had won $600 million in grants. Much of these funds came from NIH and Bill Gates, with whom they had become partners.

Despite Redfield's inglorious past, President Donald Trump put him in charge of the CDC at a time when the agency's overarching mission was promoting COVID vaccines." He "also elevated Birx, a lifelong protégée to both Redfield and Anthony Fauci and confidante to Bill Gates." These three (Redfield, Birx, and Fauci) led the White House coronavirus task force and supervised America's COVID response in the first year of the pandemic. The three of them (none of whoever treated a COVID patient—were responsible for the unreasonable lockdowns, a shutdown of the global economy, the denial of public access to available, life-saving drugs like hydroxychloroquine and ivermectin, etc. They made their draconian laws while pushing the narrative that vaccines are the only way back to normal life.

Chapter 10: More Harm than Good

The partnership of Bill Gates and Dr. Fauci had subtly hijacked the WHO's goal of curbing infectious diseases (through clean water, nutrition, and economic development) to serve their vaccine agenda. This chapter examines Gates' claim that his African and Asian vaccines yield immense public health benefits.

Ideally, a vaccine product wouldn't get licensed without undergoing "randomized placebo-controlled trials that compare health outcomes." In March 2017, I met with Dr. Fauci, Francis Collins, and a White House referee to complain that "HHS was, by then, mandating 69 doses of sixteen vaccines for America's children, none of which had ever been tested for safety against placebos before licensing." They denied this, insisting that the vaccines were safely tested, but were unable to provide any citation of using an inert placebo against a vaccine. Ten months later, HSS admitted that none of the mandated childhood vaccines had been tested. These vaccines included the best of Bill Gates" African vaccines. He has several other ineffective and dangerous vaccines in Africa.

No one can authoritatively say that Bill Gates' flagship vaccines prevent more deaths and injuries than they cause. This also means that his vaccines are experimental. He sees the continent as "a mass of human experiment with no control groups and no functional data collection systems." He suffers the same weakness of being unable to fund studies "that examine the effectiveness of their vaccines in improving health and reducing mortality." As a result, neither of them has offered empirical evidence to support their claims that their vaccines have saved millions of lives.

The idea of Africa as a mass of human experiments dates back to the colonial era. The colonial overlords, in the 1950s, opened the floodgates for pharmaceutical companies to perform vaccine experiments on millions of subjects. Since then, Pharma has maintained the culture of moving its vaccine trials to poor nations "where human guinea pigs are cheap, and even the most severe injuries will rarely delay the study." Africa, today, remains Pharma's testing ground and the place for dumping expired and defective stocks. Bill Gates has mastered the practice of collaborating with corrupt WHO officials "to scam Western donor nations into footing the bill, and guaranteeing rich profits for pharmaceutical companies in which, coincidentally, he holds hefty stock positions." The Bill and Melinda Gates Foundation, in a smooth collaboration with the WHO, has maintained the practice of human experimentation in Africa.

Malaria kills about 655,000 people annually, most of whom are African kids under the age of five. In 2010, Bill Gates "funded with $300 million a Phase III trial of GlaxoSmithKline's experimental malaria vaccine Mosquirix" which was said to be directed at young children for their developing immune system. GlaxoSmithKline contributed $500 million. NIAID contributed tens of millions. The CDC, USAID, and Wellcome Trust are other sponsors. Suspecting the vaccine may be lethal, they didn't test it against a placebo. Eventually, about 151 African infants died in the African trial, while 1,048 of the 5,049 babies suffered adverse effects such as seizures, paralysis, and convulsions. Amazingly, virologists and academics worldwide kept silent about his Mosquirix deaths, showing his influence with the virology cartel and the African governments.

In 2010, Gates funded a MenAfriVac campaign in sub-Saharan Africa in which he forcibly vaccinated thousands of children against meningitis, causing 50 of the 500 vaccinated kids to develop paralysis. Reacting to this incident, South African political economist, Professor Patrick Bond, described Gates' "philanthropic" practices as "ruthless and immoral."

Another controversial reality of Bill Gates is his keen interest in eugenics, "a racist pseudoscience that aspired to eliminate human beings deemed "unfit" in favor of the Nordic stereotypes." This view gained popularity in the early twentieth century. Gates has also expressed his obsession with population, particularly his desire to reduce earth's population. This trait is probably a family tradition as his father, "Bill Gates Sr., was a prominent corporate lawyer and civic leader in Seattle with a lifelong obsession for 'population control.'" Gates sr. headed the board of Planned Parenthood, "a neo-progressive organization founded in 1916 by the racist eugenicist Margaret Sanger to promote birth control and sterilization and to purge 'human waste.'"

Bill gates hasn't just made statements that clearly show his Dread for overpopulation, and he has investments that reflect this. On February 10, 2010, in his TED talk, he maintained that "if we do a really great job on new vaccines… we could lower (population) by perhaps

10 to fifteen percent." In his defense, his "Fact Checker" organizations argue that Gates "to suggest that lifesaving vaccines will allow more infants to survive to adulthood, thereby reassuring impoverished parents that they need not have so many children." This argument rests on the shady promise that vaccines reduce child mortality. This is a proposition that Gates doesn't demonstrate and one that isn't scientific.

Chapter 11: Hyping Phony Epidemics: "Crying Wolf"

In 1906, 800-1000 of every 1000 Americans died of infectious diseases. But, by 1976, fewer than 50 Americans per 100,000 died of contagious diseases. At this point, the CDC and NIAID became desperate to justify their enormous budgets. Hence, hyping pandemic to cause panic became the institutions' strategy. This is what most of Dr. Fauci's critics express when they criticize him for "exaggerating—and even concocting—global disease outbreaks to hype pandemic panic, elevate the biosecurity agenda, boost agency funding, promote profitable vaccines for his pharma partners, and magnify his own power."

The 1976 Swine Flu

Pharma and NIAID told Congress and Americans that the Fort Dix swine flu of 1976 was the same strain responsible for the 1918 Spanish flu, which killed 50 million people worldwide. But scientists at Fort Dix, the CDC, and HHS knew they were lying as the disease was an ordinary pig virus with no risk whatsoever for humans. They aim was to push a vaccine agenda—vaccines which the HHS and Merck conspired to rush to market. So the government launched promotional campaigns, including TV adverts, to push the agenda. But it turned out that the swine flu was not as powerful as it was all hyped to be. In a few weeks, not one case of the virus was anywhere in the world. Dr. John Anthony Morris, a senior bacteriologist, and virologist told his HHS superiors "that the flu scare was a farce and that NIAID's campaign was a boondoggle to promote a dangerous and ineffective flu vaccine for a greedy industry." But his direct superiors ordered him to stand down and "not to talk about this."

Dr. Michael Hatwick warned the HHS that the flu vaccine could cause brain injuries at the CDC. In 1976, the HHS was forced to discontinue the jab after vaccinating 49 million Americans. The vaccine was fraught with many problems, one of which was the discovery that the incidence of the flu was seven times greater in those who were vaccinated than those who weren't. The vaccine was also linked to cases of degenerative nerve disease Guillain-Barré Syndrome, paralysis, and death. Dr. Morris remained critical of the CDC's annual vaccination for the flu. He told the *Washington Post*, "It's a medical rip-off. . . . I believe the public should have truthful information based on which they can determine whether or not to take the vaccine. . . . I believe that given full information, they won't take the vaccine." But the CDC ended up silencing him like they do other dissidents. The prohibited him from publishing papers, presenting at conferences, and talking to the press. He was totally alienated from the public.

The 2005 Bird Flu

Dr. Fauci had been warning the world about the imminent bird flu since 2001. In 2004, Jeremy Farrar, Vietnam-based Oxford University Clinical Research Unit Director, identified the "the reemergence of the deadly bird flu (H5N1) in humans. The powerful Wellcome trust heavily funded the Oxford Vietnam project. Like Gates Foundation, Wellcome donates to promote the pharmaceutical industry's interests. Later, in 2020, Farrar and Bill Gates would partner "to fund modeler Neil Ferguson, the epidemiologist who produced the wildly exaggerated COVID-19 death forecasts that helped ratchet up the COVID-19 fear campaign and rationalize Draconian lockdowns." It was the same Ferguson who, in 2005, predicted that the bird flu would kill up to 150 million people. But this prediction failed massively: "only 282 people died worldwide from the disease between 2003 and 2009."

In 2005, using Ferguson's data, warned that the bird flu would kill millions of people. He argued that it was "deadly and contagious" and that it was "a time bomb waiting to go off." Pandemic expert Robert Webster, standing with Fauci, subscribed to the military vocabulary: "We have to prepare as if we were going to war—and the public needs to understand that clearly. This virus is playing its role as a natural bioterrorist." Influenced by Fauci's words, President Bush warned that "No country can afford to ignore the threat of avian flu." He would later go on to request "$1.2 billion for sufficient avian virus vaccine to inoculate 20 million Americans... $3 billion for Dr. Fauci's new seasonal flu vaccines, and $1 billion for the storage of antiviral medications." But their "fears" only turned out to be lies as the bird flu proved much less fatal than they had painted.

Observing the whole bird flu hoax, investigative journalist and attorney Michael Fumento remarked that "Dr. Fauci's recurring disease 'nightmares' often don't materialize." The same pattern of exciting pandemics characterized the 2009 Hong Kong Swine Flu, the 2016 Zika Virus, and the 2016 Dengue virus.

Chapter 12: Germ Games

The US first embarked on making large-scale offensive bioweapon research during WW1 in the spring of 1943. It was to result from a collaboration between the US military and its pharmaceutical industry partners. George W. Merck, a prominent Pharma stakeholder, led the Pentagon's bioweapons program while simultaneously directing his drug manufacturing behemoth. He once boasted "that his team could deliver biowarfare agents without vast expenditures or constructing huge facilities" and that the fact that development could proceed under the guise of legitimate medical research is another advantage of bioweapons. However, by 1969, David Franz, veteran commander of the US Army Medical Research Institute of Infectious Diseases, acknowledged that managing bioweapons was difficult to prevent accidental escapes or leakages.

Robert P. Kadlec is an American Physician and Colonel in the US Air Force. He also served as Assistant Secretary of Health and Human Services for Preparedness and Response from August 2017 until January 2021 and who managed the COVID-19 crisis during the Trump administration. Since the 1993 World Trade Center attack, he began "evangelizing about an imminent anthrax attack that would doom the American way of life." In 1999, he "organized his paranoia into several "illustrative scenarios" to demonstrate the United States' vulnerability to biological attack." In an April 2001 study for the National Defense University National War College, he suggested "the creation of a Strategic National Stockpile to warehouse countermeasures including vaccines and antibiotics, and recommended regulatory changes to provide for mandatory vaccinations and coercive quarantines in the event of a pandemic." This earned him an appointment as Special Assistant for Biodefense Planning to President George W. Bush in the immediate aftermath of the 9/11 attacks.

On Kadlec's persistent persuasion, "Congress to establish a Strategic National Stockpile, whose contents are currently worth $7 billion." He would then take over the monopoly of the stockpile purchase following the lead of Bill Gates and Dr. Fauci. In 1999, he "organized a simulation of a smallpox terrorist attack on US soil for a joint exercise by the newly formed Johns Hopkins Center for Civilian Biodefense Strategies and the Department of

Health & Human Services (HHS)." His simulation and several others would follow it (most of whom were championed by Bill Gates). Bill Gates would sponsor simulations presided over at the John Hopkins center in the next few decades. But none of these simulations had the protection of public health in view.

The 9/11 attacks rekindled US interests in germ warfare. This opened up opportunities to pharma and all stakeholders. As a result, the US biodefense budget went from $137 million in 1997 to $14.5 billion for 2001–2004. Between 2001 and 2014, the US had spent over $80 billion on biodefense. But since germ weaponry was still illegal, vaccines were "a critical euphemism for the revival of the multibillion-dollar bioweapons industry." This stirred the need for research. Consequently, by 2004, NIAID had been transformed into an arm of the defense sector, making Dr. Fauci a major player in the germ and biodefense project.

Besides, at this time, "rising biosecurity cartel adopted simulations as signaling mechanisms for choreographing lockstep response among corporate, political, and military technocrats charged with managing global exigencies." Most of these scenario planning employ "strategies familiar to anyone who has read the CIA's notorious psychological warfare manuals for shattering indigenous societies, obliterating traditional economics and social bonds, for using imposed isolation and the demolition of traditional economies to crush resistance, to foster chaos, demoralization, dependence, and fear, and for imposing centralized and autocratic governance." University of Wisconsin historian Alfred W. McCoy suggests that the CIA funded the Yale obedience experiments were intended to control human behavior.

According to McCoy, one of the facts from this research was on isolation's effect on the brain. It is said to "affect organic brain development, and the human body, length of life, cardiovascular health, and so on. For example, social isolation doubles the risk of death in Blacks while increasing the risk of early death in Caucasians by 60–84 percent." Several more simulations and research went on over the years with improvements in practicability and feasibility.

In May 2018, Bill Gates created "a kind of permanent standing committee called the Global Preparedness Monitoring Board (GPMB), including some of the most powerful global public health kingpins, to institutionalize the lessons derived from all these scenario planning drills. This global committee would serve as the authoritative body to impose rules during the coming pandemic. Then, in June 2019, twenty weeks before the COVID-19 crises, "Dr. Michael Ryan, executive director of the WHO's health emergencies program, summarized the conclusions of GPMB's pandemic report, warning that "we are entering a new phase of high impact epidemics" that would constitute "a new normal" where governments worldwide would strengthen control and restrict the mobility of citizens."

At this point, it now made sense why Kadlec had, for twenty years, been writing about using a pandemic to overcome democracy. The latest, as of then, the 2019 Crimson Contagion simulation, served "to evangelize state-level health bureaucracies, municipal officials, hospital and law enforcement agencies across America with the messages developed in the preceding simulations." Two months after the Crimson Contagion and three weeks after US intelligence agencies believed the COVID-19 had begun in Wuhan, the Bill-Gates-led *Event 201* simulation took place. It "was as close as one could get to a "real-time" simulation. It was a meeting of a hypothetical Pandemic Emergency Board in the same week that COVID-19 was already claiming its first victims in Wuhan." Its theme "was that such a crisis would prove an opportunity to promote new vaccines and tighten information and behavioral controls through propaganda, censorship, and surveillance."

In the light of all these, the COVID-19 has been described by several scholars as a military project. Dr. Fauci, Bill Gates, Robert P. Kadlec, the Big Pharma, the CIA, et al. had carefully orchestrated.

Discussion Questions

- Why was the idea of compelling the use of masks, social distancing, and lockdowns at the beginning of the COVID-19 pandemic unscientific?

- Doctors that offered dissenting views from Dr. Fauci were punished and silenced. How?

- How did Pharma profit from public health?

- What is the PIs? What's their significance to Dr. Fauci, Pharma, etc.?

- The idea that science is fixed and we all have to just follow the authorities is wrong. Why?

- Explain the phrase, "Science is disruptive."

- Professor Peter Duesberg was a scapegoat and victim of Dr. Fauci's medical totalitarianism. How?

- How is many African countries a victim of the corruption in Big Pharma?

- There is reason to believe that the COVID-19 pandemic was planned. Why?

Thank you for choosing this book! If you enjoyed reading, please support us by giving us your five-star ratings/reviews. You may also like to get these other related book summaries from us:

SUMMARY

Of

Dr. Joseph Mercola
& Ronnie Cummins'

The Truth About COVID-19

Exposing The Great Reset, Lockdowns, Vaccine Passports, and the New Normal

Crystal Publishing

SUMMARY

Of

Daniel G. Amen's

The End *of* **Mental Illness**

How Neuroscience is Transforming Psychiatry and Helping Prevent or Reverse Mood and Anxiety Disorders, ADHD Addiction, PTSD, Psychosis Personality Disorders and more.

Crystal Publishing

Made in the USA
Columbia, SC
29 March 2022

58300289R00030